Simply
COARSE
FISHING

Written and Ilustrated by

Tony Whieldon

ELLESMERE
THE MEDLAR PRESS
2009

Published by the Medlar Press Limited,
The Grange, Ellesmere, Shropshire.
www.medlarpress.com

ISBN 978-1-899600-90-8

Designed and produced in England by
The Medlar Press Limited, Ellesmere.

CONTENTS

FOREWORD 5

THE FISH 7

FISH SPECIES 9

FLOAT FISHING 21
  Plumbing the Depth 22
  Float Rods 23
  Types of Float 24

LEDGERING 39
  Ledger Rod and Tackle 40
  Ledger Rigs 42
  Using a Quivertip 43

LAKE FISHING 45

RIVER FISHING 49

CANAL FISHING 55

BAITS 57
  Loose Feed and Groundbait 61

PLAYING AND LANDING 62

UNHOOKING AND RETURNING 64

REELS 68

SPECIMEN RODS 69

HOOKS 70

LINE 72

PIKE LEDGER RIG 74

FISHING LOG 75

FOREWORD

Chris Yates

When, as a wildly keen eleven year old, I first went fishing, the only guides I had were Mr Green, my angling neighbour - who I hardly ever saw because, naturally, he was always by the river - and a how-to-fish booklet that I bought for sixpence in the local pet shop. Though it was very elementary, I loved it firstly because of the surprisingly well drawn pen and ink illustrations and secondly because of the hope it inspired by such confident statements as 'perch will always take a worm' and 'carp can be caught on bread'. It did not tell me how to fish the worm or the bread, but that didn't seem to matter at the time. I thought as long as I kept the bait in the water I was bound to succeed in the end, which was true in a way, but I had to wait an awfully long time, especially for the carp.

How much better it would have been if I had somehow conjured an advance (*fifty* years in advance!) copy of Tony Whieldon's wonderful little book. Within these pages there are not only some very fine illustrations but also many extremely clear descriptions instructing the novice just *how* to fish the various baits, or tackle the various kinds of water. The profiles of the different species are succinctly written and the advice on floats and float fishing is particularly well done; but all of it, as the book's title states, is made simple and understandable, even to a technophobe like me. The only real similarity between my sixpenny guide and this far superior edition are the gridded pages of the fishing log at the end. When I first began angling it was always wonderful whenever I had a reason to fill in a section with details of a capture, but the pages remained blank for many months. If I had only had a guide as good as this I could have filled in the whole log before the end of my first season . . .

Chris Yates

THE FISH

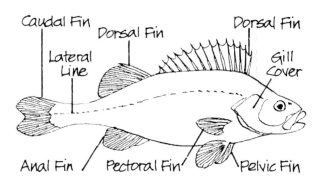

Fish need oxygen to survive. This is extracted from the water via the gills which consist of thin, feathery blood vessels beneath a thin membrane.

All fish have a covering of mucus as a barrier against infection. Overlapping scales protect the fish's muscles but also permit the fish to flex its body as they are only fixed at the front.

The lateral line is a very efficient sensory system which can detect any changes in pressure around the fish.

ROACH

Roach are everywhere. Rivers, lakes, ponds, canals and fenland drains all contain this gregarious fish. Although mainly a bottom feeder, roach will also feed in mid-water and also, at times, right on the surface.

They eat insect larvae, molluscs, small crustaceans, worms and weed. Mild, overcast days, or as the light fades at dusk, usually prompt roach to feed confidently. They often roll on the surface, over the feeding area.

PERCH

Small perch are widely distributed and usually swim in packs close to weedbeds. They feed on insect larvae and fish fry, but as they grow larger, feed almost entirely on small fish, perch included.

Big perch adopt a more solitary existence, lying up near some feature from where they ambush their prey. Small fry, scattering on the surface, will betray the presence of a feeding perch pack beneath.

CRUCIAN CARP

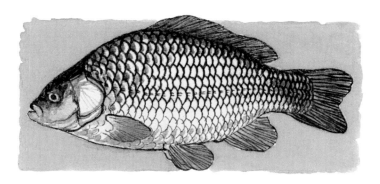

This small carp lives in heavily —
weeded lakes and ponds. It feeds
mostly on the bottom on a diet of
bloodworm, snails, crustaceans and
underwater vegetation.

Unlike the common carp, it has
no mouth barbels. Crucians tend to
feed more during the mornings and
evenings and also after dark.

Large lakes with a rich food supply
will produce good specimens but small
ponds may be overrun with a stunted
population.

CHUB

Chub are widespread in most big rivers. Some small rivers also hold surprisingly large specimens. They also exist in some canals and lakes.

Overhanging foliage, weir pools and streamy runs are all places where they like to shoal up. Very large specimens tend to be less gregarious and lie up in deep holes under the bank and tree roots.

Chub will eat anything. Insects and their larvae, shrimps, snails, crayfish, frogs, fish, slugs and berries are just a few examples.

EEL

Eels spawn somewhere between the Azores and the Bahamas. The larvae make an incredible journey lasting three years, until they arrive at an estuary. They then start to migrate upstream, fanning out into tributaries and other types of water.

During its six to ten year period in freshwater the eel will feed on larvae, nymphs and small fish. Eels are especially active at night or during overcast thundery weather conditions.

PIKE

Pike are widespread in lowland lakes and rivers, especially where weed is abundant. The sub-surface plants provide good cover for the pike as it waits in ambush.

Fish are the pike's main source of food but frogs, voles and young water fowl also feature on the menu from time to time.

Reservoirs which are regularly well stocked with trout produce very big pike, and the limestone lakes of Ireland are a mecca for this fish—chomping predator.

RUDD

This beautiful fish is predominantly a surface feeder and prefers weedy lakes, ponds, canals and backwaters.

Rudd feed on insects in the surface film and larvae beneath the surface, and at times will feed on the bottom. Shoals can often be seen feeding close to the bank, alongside sedge or weedbeds.

Small rudd are generally silver on the flanks but larger specimens are often a brassy colour with vivid crimson fins.

TENCH

Slow flowing rivers, canals and lakes are home to this chunky beauty. When the water temperature rises, tench start to root around on the bottom in search of bloodworms and snails.

This activity often produces tiny bubbles on the surface, sometimes referred to as 'needle bubbles'. Tench feed early in the morning or during the evening, but if the weather is overcast may feed throughout the day. They will often roll on the surface over an area where they are feeding.

BREAM

Lakes, reservoirs, meres, canals, drains and slow rivers are home to this most positive of bottom feeders. Bream form shoals (smaller fish in large shoals and large fish in small shoals) and follow regular routes when feeding.

This is another fish that will roll on the surface over a feeding area. They also produce bubbles when feeding, accompanied by much discoloration of the water.

COMMON CARP

The common carp and its cultivated varieties, mirror carp and leather carp, are all the same species and share the same breeding and feeding habits.

They thrive in lakes where weed is abundant, and some rivers and canals also hold a few. Insect larvae, snails, crustaceans and weed form the main diet which is rooted out from the bottom. Feeding activity will disturb the area so much that large patches of water will quickly become coloured.

BARBEL

This powerful, streamlined river fish thrives in well-oxygenated water such as that found in weirpools and runs over gravel.

Barbel are exclusively bottom feeders, searching out morsels with their sensitive barbels around the mouth. Most concentrated feeding takes place at dusk and after dark. Insect larvae, snails, crustaceans and small fish are readily consumed by this underwater vacuum cleaner.

Barbel have also been stocked into a few gravel pits with some success.

DACE

Although this little silver fish can be found in some lakes, it is mainly a resident of running water. Even small streams can produce (what would be classed as large) fish of 14-15 oz., with the occassional 1 lb specimen.

Dace form large shoals and dimple the water surface as they feed on insects. They are sometimes mistaken for small chub - look at the anal fin for positive identification.

DACE   CHUB

FLOAT FISHING

Most anglers would agree that float fishing is the most enjoyable way of catching a fish. However, there is no such thing as a float for all occasions.

Over the years, modification in design based on experience has resulted in recognised patterns to cope with the variety of conditions.

The selection of multi-coloured creations in many anglers' boxes may confuse the beginner. But a closer analysis will show that there are only a few main groups backed up by the odd special design for extreme needs.

PLUMBING THE DEPTH

Thread the float on to the line and connect the hooklength and hook. Estimate the depth and fix the float. Attach the plummet and lob the tackle into the fishing area. To obtain an accurate reading, the line must be slack between the float and the rod tip. When all is correct, fix required shot.

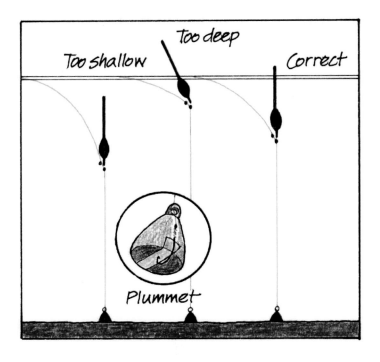

FLOAT ROD

A float rod needs to be long. Both from the point of view of trotting a stick float or fishing a deep lake swim, a long rod will make all the difference.

A long rod will provide a lot more control when the line needs mending or a float needs to be set very deep, without the need to resort to a slider.

A rod with a progressive action is very versatile, being able to cope with fast-biting small fish and having the backbone to tame bigger specimens.

Good lengths for a float rod are 12, 13 or, best of all, 14 feet.

STICKS

These lightweight, elegant river floats are perfect for trotting a small bait in evenly-flowing water. They are fastened to the line by short lengths of silicone tubing, top and bottom, with an extra piece in the centre, if needed. They work best with at least six shot on the line. The shot can then be moved quickly for different presentation.

Most sticks have a balsa body and heavy wood stem to aid stability. A wire stem stick will give even more stability when conditions are blustery.

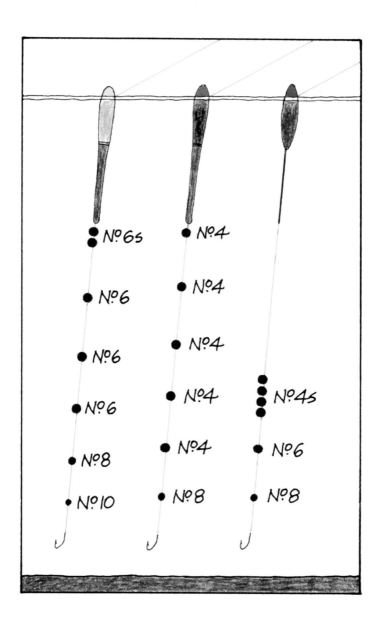

AVONS

Originally, these river floats were made with a crow quill stem and a cork body. Nowadays, they are made with a variety of material such as cane, balsa, wire and plastic but still have the traditional profile.

Used in conjunction with a centrepin reel, these are the ideal floats for trotting a bait through long, streamy areas of water.

They are fastened to the line in the same manner as stickfloats and balsas, with silicone float bands.

BALSAS

These buoyant floats
are used in swims which
are too brawly for the
lighter stick floats.
As the name suggests
they are made entirely
of balsa wood and
are attached to the
line, top and bottom.
The largest balsas
are known as chubbers
and used to fish large
baits such as bread,
meat and lobworms in
turbulent swims, quite
often at long range.
They are especially useful
when the river is running higher
than normal, after heavy rain. Chubbers
are also made in transparent plastic
which is useful in very clear water.

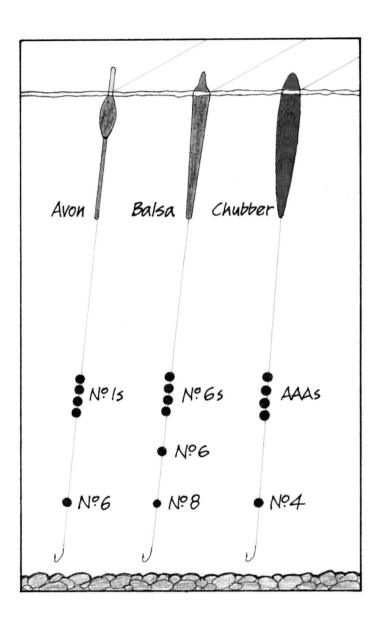

Avon Balsa Chubber

Nº 1s Nº 6s AAAs

Nº 6

Nº 6 Nº 8 Nº 4

WAGGLERS

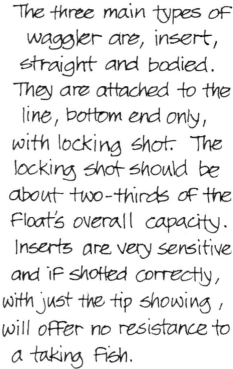

The three main types of waggler are, insert, straight and bodied. They are attached to the line, bottom end only, with locking shot. The locking shot should be about two-thirds of the float's overall capacity. Inserts are very sensitive and if shotted correctly, with just the tip showing, will offer no resistance to a taking fish.

Straights are more visible in choppy water and will anchor a bait if needed. Bodied wagglers, because of their greater capacity, permit longer casts.

Wagglers must always be fished with a sunken line. Here is the procedure, after the float has hit the water.

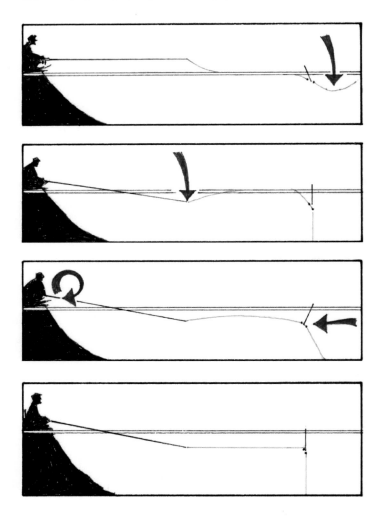

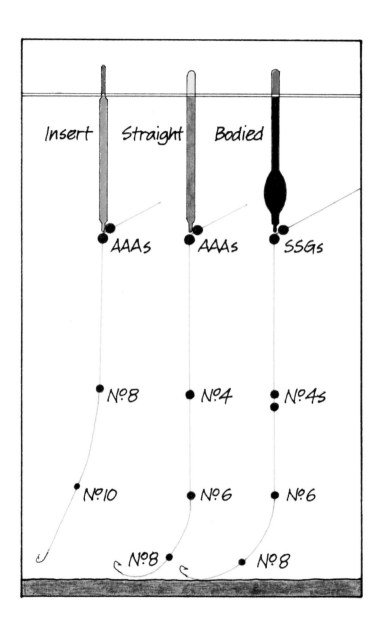

Insert   Straight   Bodied

AAAs   AAAs   SSGs

Nº8   Nº4   Nº4s

Nº10   Nº6   Nº6

            Nº8   Nº8

SLIDERS

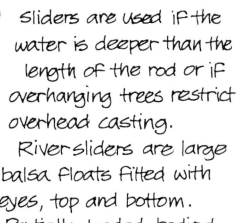

Sliders are used if the water is deeper than the length of the rod or if overhanging trees restrict overhead casting.

River sliders are large balsa floats fitted with eyes, top and bottom. Partially-loaded bodied wagglers make the best sliders for stillwater work.

The success of any slider depends on a well tied stop knot.

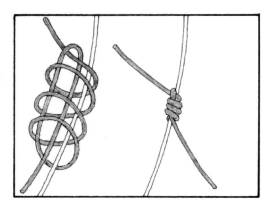

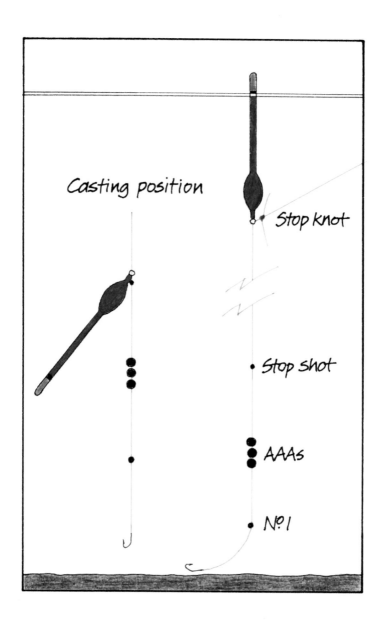

Casting position

Stop knot

Stop shot

AAAs

Nº1

DRIFTBEATER AND TRENT TROTTER

When surface drift is bad, the odd-looking driftbeater will keep things stable.

The tip is visible, even in choppy water. It is locked to the line waggler fashion and should be fished well overdepth.

The stumpy little Trent trotter comes into its own in shallow, fast flowing water. As it is fished on a sunk line, it can be trotted well beyond the rod tip without the need to keep mending the line.

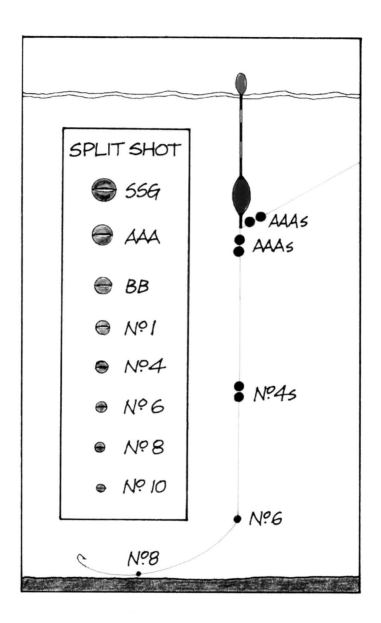

SPLIT SHOT

- SSG
- AAA
- BB
- Nº 1
- Nº 4
- Nº 6
- Nº 8
- Nº 10

AAAs
AAAs
Nº4s
Nº6
Nº8

THE LIFT METHOD

The effectiveness of this method hinges entirely on accurate plumbing, for the distance between the float and the shot should be exactly the same as the depth of the water.

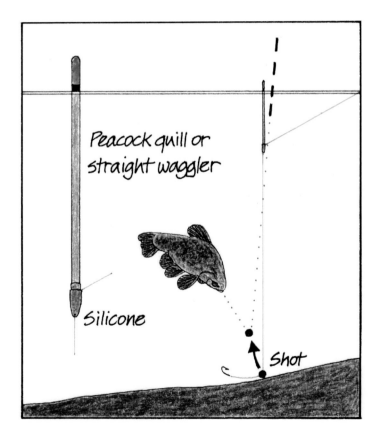

Peacock quill or straight waggler

Silicone

Shot

SURFACE RIG

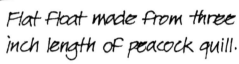

Flat float made from three inch length of peacock quill.

Hooklength

Optional shot

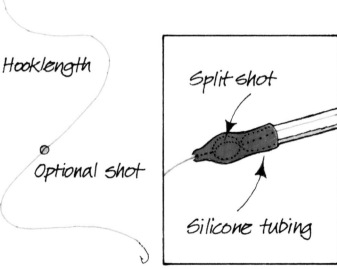

Split shot

Silicone tubing

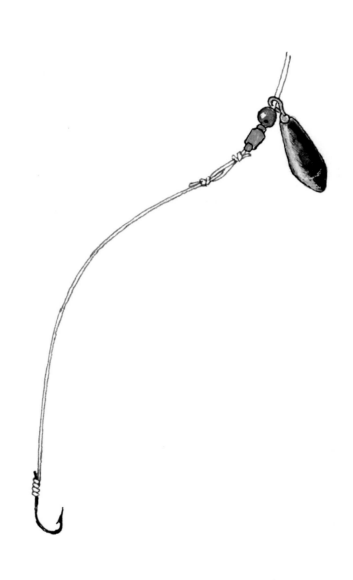

LEDGERING

Where a long cast is needed or if a bait needs to be anchored on the bottom, sometimes in a current, then that is the time to use ledger tackle. A ledger can also be used at close range and is a useful option if bad weather conditions render float fishing impractical.

This is a method which accounts for a lot of large fish, but then large fish spend a lot of time close to the bottom anyway.

LEDGER ROD

Ledger rods range from wand-like affairs up to the more meaty models for use with large feeders.

Most have interchangeable, push on quiver tips, varying in sensitivity, for coping with different conditions.

The ideal model is one that will perform well with both bomb and feeder.

A useful companion to this rod is a target board which will make bites a lot easier to see.

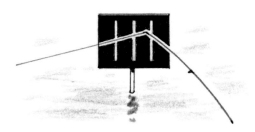

LEDGER TACKLE

The items of terminal tackle shown below are the most commonly used. Open-end feeders are used for groundbait mixes, block-end feeders for maggots. Ledger stops are preferable to split shot as they do not damage the line. Drilled bullets are good for rolling ledgers, and bombs for casting.

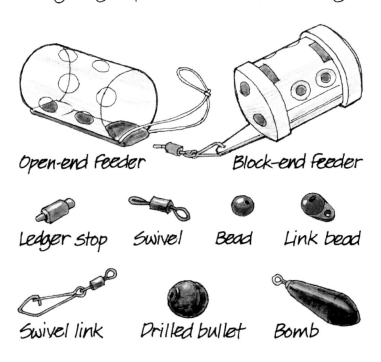

Open-end feeder   Block-end feeder

Ledger stop   Swivel   Bead   Link bead

Swivel link   Drilled bullet   Bomb

LEDGER RIGS

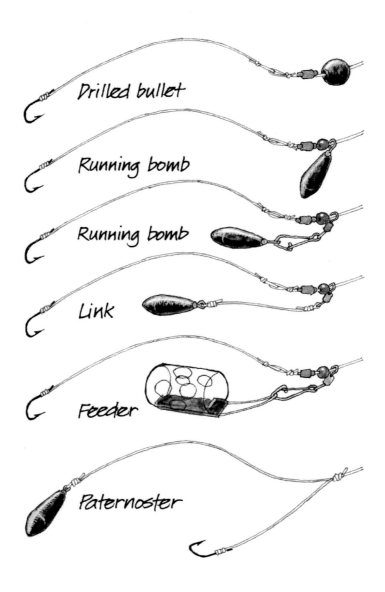

Drilled bullet

Running bomb

Running bomb

Link

Feeder

Paternoster

USING A QUIVERTIP

The quivertip is a very sensitive bite indicator for still and running water.

Position of rod to overcome the pressure of mid-stream current, when the far bank is being fished.

Drop back bite

Normal set-up

Fishing with a feeder and quiver tip is a very popular form of ledgering on larger rivers.

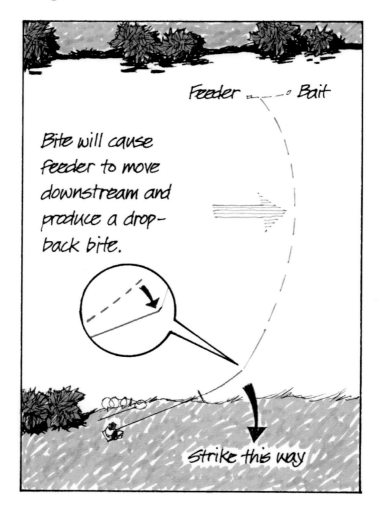

Feeder - - - - Bait

Bite will cause feeder to move downstream and produce a drop-back bite.

Strike this way

LAKE FISHING

The first rule to remember when it comes to fishing a lake is that fish are not spread evenly throughout the water. Time spent making a survey is time well spent. Signs to look for are, areas of discoloured water, fish rolling on the surface, bubbles rising to the surface – sure indications that fish are feeding in that area.

Other ways of locating fish are by using features, a selection of which are shown on the following page.

Fishing into the wind is always worth
a try provided the wind is not cold.
When wind blows over a lake, surface
water moves in the same direction as
the wind. When it comes into contact
with a shoreline, the water doubles
back beneath the surface flow. This
sudden transition disturbs food items
which, in turn, attracts feeding fish.

SURFACE FLOW ➡

⬅ UNDERTOW

LIKELY LAKE HOTSPOTS

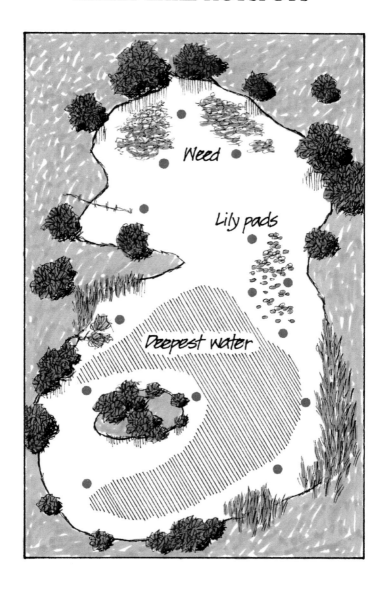

MARGIN FISHING

Margins can often be the best areas to fish in a lake. If the water is coloured as it often is in heavily – stocked carp and tench waters, the fish will feed throughout the day.

Free offerings of bait will get them going, then a simple lift bite float rig can be lowered into the bait area.

At dusk and after dark, large carp patrol the margins of lakes. They can be ambushed with a floating bait suspended beneath the rod tip.

RIVER FISHING

Small rivers are best tackled with the mobile approach as fish can easily be spooked in confined swims. Large seat boxes and rod holdalls would be too cumbersome. A fishing waistcoat to carry items of tackle, rod, landing net and a light, collapsible chair is far more practical.

Large rivers, however, can be tackled with a far more laid back attitude. Swims are larger, and provided they are sensibly supplied with loose feed (if needed) they will produce fish of all sorts throughout the day.

LIKELY RIVER HOTSPOTS

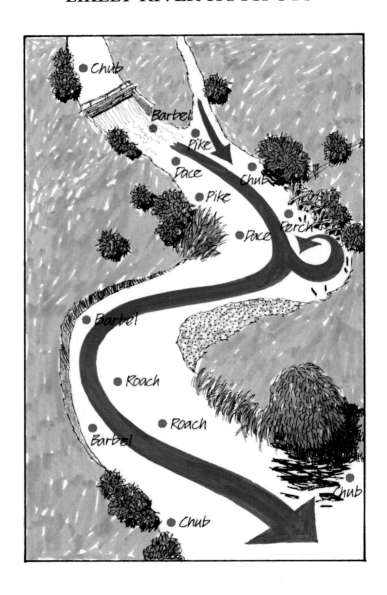

TROTTING THE STREAM

It's best to stand up for this method as it gives more control over the stick, balsa or Avon float. The ideal line for a float to trot is directly downstream from the rod tip.

A long rod will generally achieve this and lessen the need to keep mending the line.

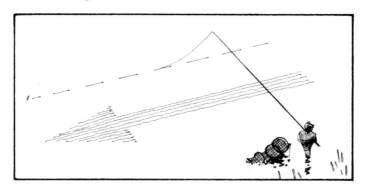

A trotted float should be allowed to go with the current, but kept in check on a fairly tight line; and at times, held back so that the bait rides up in the water.

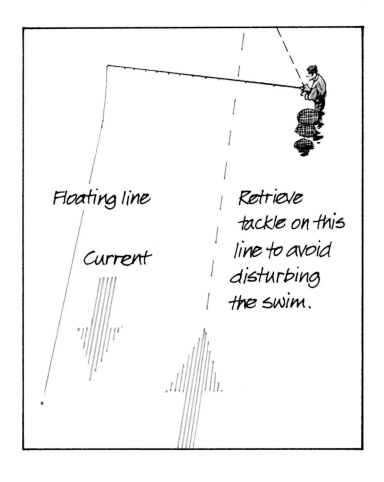

Floating line

Current

Retrieve tackle on this line to avoid disturbing the swim.

MENDING THE LINE

When a float is trotted downstream on a line beyond the tip of the rod, there is often a tendency for the line to develop a bow. If this is not dealt with, the float will be dragged off course, across the current.

The remedy is to trap the line on the reel and lift the rod tip through an arc. This may have to be done more than once during a trot down.

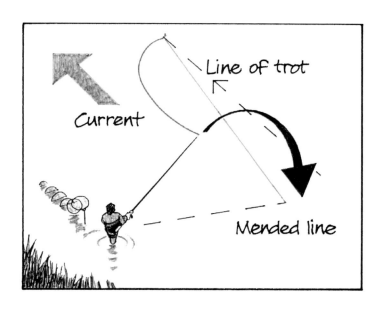

Line of trot

Current

Mended line

USING A BAITDROPPER

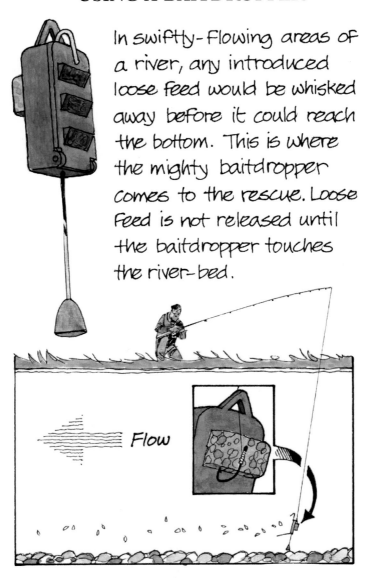

In swiftly-flowing areas of a river, any introduced loose feed would be whisked away before it could reach the bottom. This is where the mighty baitdropper comes to the rescue. Loose feed is not released until the baitdropper touches the river-bed.

Flow

CANAL FISHING

Some canals may not look inspiring, but they can be full of surprises. Even those in urban surroundings are capable of producing really good bags. However, the choice is unlimited with many miles of fishing in rural bliss.

Boats, pedestrians and cyclists can be a problem at some locations, during summer. Autumn and winter then, are the best times to fish such places.

Feeding more than one line on a canal swim is a sensible approach. One line can suddenly dry up or be disturbed by a passing boat, so it's good to have another option.

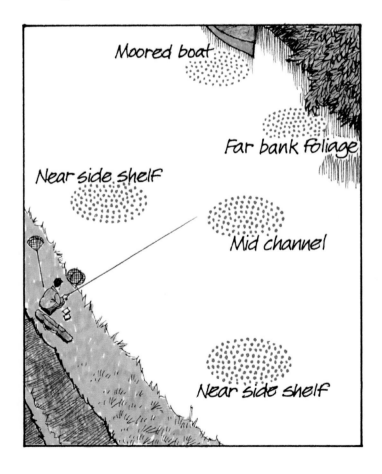

BAITS

MAGGOTS   The most widely used bait. Large white maggots make good hookbaits. Pinkies are much smaller and are used on small hooks for shy fish, or as feed, and in groundbait. Squatts are tiny and used solely as feed, or in groundbait.

CASTERS   Maggots (larvae) turn into casters (pupae). Newly formed casters are pale in colour and gradually deepen with time. Pale casters sink in water. As they darken, they become more buoyant. Very dark casters actually float.

Store maggots in bran or sawdust, in deep sided, open top containers in a fridge. This will keep them fresh and stop them turning to casters.

BREAD PASTE Bread in all its forms is a cheap and versatile bait. Paste is simply a mixture of bread and water which is kneaded into the required consistency.

BREAD FLAKE Pinch out a piece of bread from the inside of a loaf and fold it around a hook. Squeeze the area over the hook shank and it's ready to use.

BREAD CRUST Cut through the crust of an unsliced white loaf. Prise out the crust with some flake attached for a very buoyant bait.

PUNCHED BREAD When used with very small hooks, these tiny compressed pellets can bring a swim back to life.

Bread Punch

WORMS Lobworms, redworms and brandlings are the three main types of earthworm used by anglers. Lobworms are the largest and can be used whole, for large fish, or cut into sections. The tail of a lobworm is very effective. Redworms and brandlings can be found in large numbers in well rotted manure and compost.

BLOODWORMS   These lively, blood red little wrigglers are the larvae of the chironomid midge. They live in the bottom sediment of ponds and lakes and can also be seen in water butts.

To present them properly requires the use of very small hooks. Bloodworms work extremely well in winter and are a favourite with match fishermen.

HEMPSEED The smell of this oily seed makes it a good feed bait. It can also be used on the hook with devastating results.

SWEETCORN What nicer bait could there be? It's delicious. During the summer, it works well for larger fish.

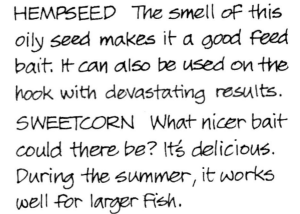

LUNCHEON MEAT A smelly and very effective bait. It can also be cut into strips rather than cubes. Best used with a wide gape hook.

MIXERS These little dog biscuits make a good buoyant bait. They need to be soaked in water before mounting on the hook.

CHEESE This can be kneaded into a paste or mixed with bread paste. Cheese hardens in water so the hookpoint should be exposed.

LOOSE FEED AND GROUNDBAIT

Loose feed is introduced to the swim during the act of fishing. It usually consists of samples of hook bait. It can be fed by hand, catapult or bait dropper, if the current is strong. Little and often is the best way to loose feed.

Groundbait is made from brown crumb, or a mixture of brown and white crumb and water. It can be used on its own or with samples, eg., maggots, hemp, sweet corn, chopped worms etc. Ready – made continental mixes are available.

Introduce groundbait carefully from the start and build up if need be.

PLAYING AND LANDING

Once a fish is hooked, always keep
an angle between the rod and the
line. This will have the effect of
using the rod as a shock absorber.
Holding the rod tip high will achieve
this effect, and the visible line will
show in which direction the fish is
moving. Never point the rod at the fish!

Always keep the line tight and if
the fish makes a strong run let him
go, but grudgingly, by using a pre-
set clutch or by added finger
pressure on the reel. The best way
to turn a fish is by side strain.
If a fish starts running in, recover
line rapidly.

When a fish begins to tire, its runs will become shorter until, eventually, it turns on its side. This is the time to reach for the landing net.

Immerse the head of the net in the water and draw the fish over the net. Never jab at the fish with the net. When the fish is lying well over the net, lift the frame clear of the water and pull the net in horizontally.

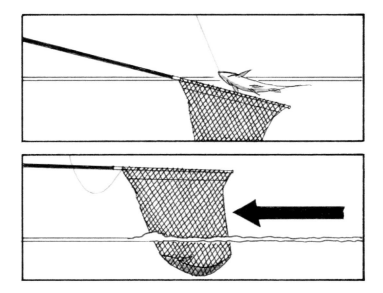

UNHOOKING AND RETURNING

Small hooks can be removed cleanly with the aid of a disgorger. Slide the tool down the hooklength and push on the hook. Withdraw the disgorger with the hook inside.

Larger hooks, especially those used for pike can be extracted with artery forceps. When handling fish, always ensure hands are wet. Large fish should be laid on a wet unhooking mat when hooks are being removed.

Never keep too many fish in a keepnet, and never common carp. The carp has a strong dorsal fin spine which can snag the mesh and may cause injury to the fish. Fish can be released from a keepnet simply by lowering the opening of the net into the water to let them swim free.

Weighing and photographing large fish should be done without delay. A wet sling should be used to weigh the fish. Once confined to the dark interior of the sling, the fish should lie still to give an accurate reading on the scales.

After the stress of fighting against the resistance of the rod and the period of being weighed and, perhaps photographed, a large fish will probably need some help when it is reintroduced to the water.

This is done by the angler, who supports the fish in an upright position until it swims away of its own accord.

River fish should always be held with their heads facing upstream.

STAKING OUT A KEEPNET

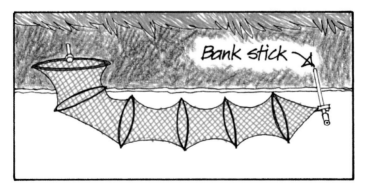

REELS

The most commonly used reel is the fixed spool. It is easy to use and will produce extremely long casts if correctly loaded with good line.

The closed face reel is very popular with match fishermen. The line is completely protected which guarantees tangle-proof casts in windy weather.

The centrepin is the ideal reel for trotting a float downstream, but it takes a lot of getting used to. However, there's nothing quite like the feel of a big fish, on a centrepin.

SPECIMEN RODS

If pike, large carp or big eels are the quarry, a rod with a test curve of at least 2lb will be needed. Lines of 10-15 lb breaking strain are used in conjunction with this beefy fish tamer.

This type of rod is capable of producing extremely long casts, swinging out large pike baits and bullying big fish away from snags.

HOOKS

Hooks can be bought loose or ready-tied to a nylon monofilament hook-length. There are many different designs and they run in size from the minute 24 up to the size 2.

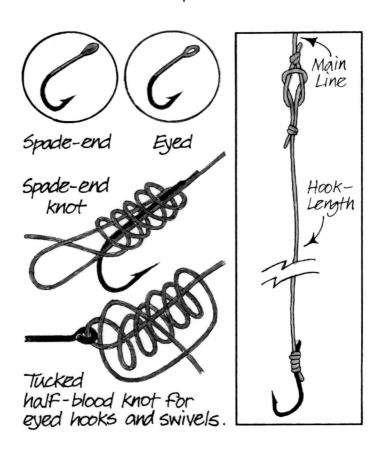

Spade-end

Eyed

Spade-end knot

Tucked half-blood knot for eyed hooks and swivels.

Main Line

Hook-Length

HOOKLENGTHS

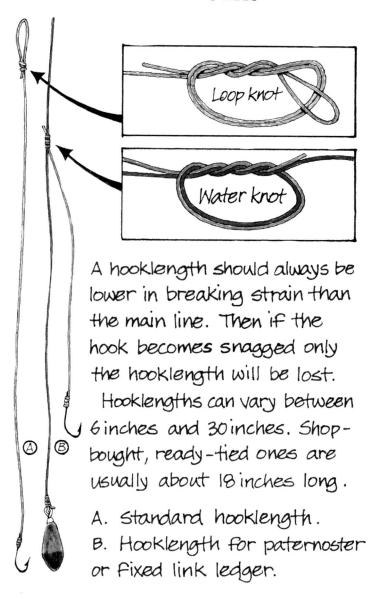

Loop knot

Water knot

A hooklength should always be lower in breaking strain than the main line. Then if the hook becomes snagged only the hooklength will be lost.

Hooklengths can vary between 6 inches and 30 inches. Shop-bought, ready-tied ones are usually about 18 inches long.

A. Standard hooklength.
B. Hooklength for paternoster or fixed link ledger.

LINE

2½lb (1·10kg) is a suitable line for
float fishing for roach, dace, rudd,
perch and small chub. Larger fish
would obviously warrant something
stronger, especially where weed and
snags are present. Here, 4lb (1·80kg)
to 6lb (2·70kg) would be advisable.
Large carp, pike and large eels will
require line of between 8lb (3·50kg)
and 15lb (7kg), depending on the
amount of snags in the water.

Knots for
connecting
line to reel
spool.

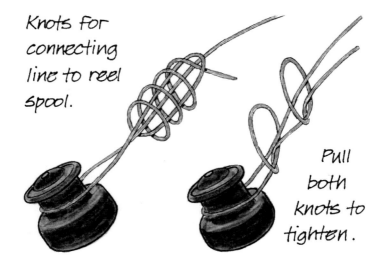

Pull
both
knots to
tighten.

FEATHERING THE LINE

This is simply checking the speed at which line leaves the reel spool when a cast is made. It will ensure that the terminal tackle precedes a waggler float just before it touches down. It also helps in a cross wind to prevent too much bow developing in the line when a long cast is made.

PIKE LEDGER RIG

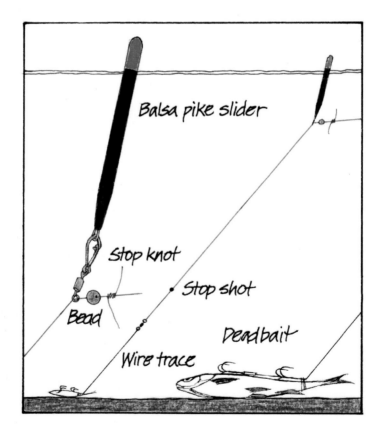

Balsa pike slider

Stop knot

Stop shot

Bead

Deadbait

Wire trace

FISHING LOG

DATE	VENUE	FISH CAUGHT	WEIGHT	NOTES

FISHING LOG

DATE	VENUE	FISH CAUGHT	WEIGHT	NOTES

FISHING LOG

DATE	VENUE	FISH CAUGHT	WEIGHT	NOTES

FISHING LOG

DATE	VENUE	FISH CAUGHT	WEIGHT	NOTES

FISHING LOG

DATE	VENUE	FISH CAUGHT	WEIGHT	NOTES

FISHING LOG

DATE	VENUE	FISH CAUGHT	WEIGHT	NOTES

If you have enjoyed this book you might
be interested in the other fishing books
at www.medlarpress.com

Tight Lines!